CW01149529

Original title:
Love's Guiding Light

Copyright © 2024 Swan Charm
All rights reserved.

Author: Swan Charm
ISBN HARDBACK: 978-9916-86-842-3
ISBN PAPERBACK: 978-9916-86-843-0
ISBN EBOOK: 978-9916-86-844-7

**Rays of Cherished Moments**

In mornings bright and clear,
Whispers of laughter near.
Sunlight spills on the ground,
Joyful echoes all around.

Time dances on the breeze,
Fleeting joys that aim to please.
Memories wrapped in gold,
Stories of love that unfold.

Through trees where shadows play,
We find our hearts' own way.
Moments stitched with care,
In every smile we share.

As sunlight starts to fade,
We gather the love we made.
Let's hold these rays so tight,
Guided by the soft twilight.

In every cherished glance,
Life offers us a chance.
To live in these sweet days,
In the warmth of golden rays.

## Paths Aligned in Glow

Underneath the starry sky,
We walk where silence lies.
Footsteps soft on the trail,
In whispers, dreams prevail.

The moonlight paints our way,
Guiding us through night and day.
With every breath we take,
New bonds form, old ones wake.

In harmony we stride,
With the universe as guide.
Each step a rhythm shared,
Paths aligned, hearts declared.

Through the shadows and the light,
We find truth in every sight.
Journey leads to brighter days,
In the glow, we dance and sway.

Together, come what may,
With love to light the way.
In every moment shown,
The paths we tread, our own.

## The Firefly Dance

In the dusk, they arise,
Little stars in disguise.
Flickering, darting near,
They paint the night sincere.

A gentle buzzing sound,
Magic all around.
They twirl in joyful flight,
Flashes of pure delight.

Carrying wishes low,
In their shimmering glow.
With each spark and each gleam,
They weave a glowing dream.

Lost in their fleeting show,
The heart begins to grow.
In the night's embrace they prance,
Nature's own sweet romance.

With every glow they lend,
Dreams are broken, then mend.
So we dance, light and free,
In the firefly jubilee.

# **Threads of Light and Heart**

In the tapestry of night,
Threads weave from dark to light.
Every color has a tale,
In the loom where dreams prevail.

Gentle hands in the weave,
Soft whispers we believe.
Patterns of joy appear,
Stitched with hope, love, and cheer.

Brighter hues come alive,
With every spark we thrive.
In the fabric of our days,
Life's threads dance in sweet ways.

As shadows gently spin,
The heart knows where to begin.
In each stitch, a feeling shared,
In the warmth, we are bared.

With every thread we tie,
We find truth, never shy.
In this web, we embark,
Threads of light in the dark.

## When Hearts Illuminate

In shadows deep, we find our way,
With whispers soft, the night turns gray.
Hearts aflame, they pulse with light,
Guiding souls through endless night.

A gentle touch, a knowing glance,
In silence shared, our spirits dance.
Together strong, we face the storm,
In darkest hours, our love keeps warm.

Through winding paths, our journey flows,
In every breath, our essence grows.
With every beat, the cosmos sings,
A melody that freely brings.

As stars align, we chase our dreams,
With courage bold, or so it seems.
Hand in hand, we'll forge ahead,
In this bright realm where hope is fed.

And when the world begins to fade,
Our love will rise, its light displayed.
For in our hearts, a spark ignites,
Illuminating endless nights.

# Dancing with the Dawn

As morning breaks, the skies reveal,
A gentle hush, a vibrant feel.
With every ray that kisses land,
The world awakens, hand in hand.

The golden hues, they start to glow,
In fields of dreams, our spirits flow.
With laughter sweet, we twirl and spin,
Embracing light as day begins.

The breeze it carries whispered tunes,
As flowers bloom beneath the moons.
We leap with joy, our hearts so free,
In this ballet of you and me.

With every step, the shadows lie,
And hope ascends to paint the sky.
For in this dance, our souls unite,
Creating warmth that feels so right.

So let us dance, embrace the morn,
A symphony of love reborn.
In every sunrise, dreams will flaunt,
Together here, our hearts will taunt.

## **Illuminated Paths**

In twilight's embrace, we wander slow,
Footsteps whisper secrets, soft and low.
Each star a promise, guiding our way,
Through shadows and light, we seize the day.

A flicker in the distance, hope ignites,
Leading us forward, through endless nights.
Together we traverse, hand in hand,
On illuminated paths, where dreams expand.

## The Glow Between Us

In the silence, a warmth starts to rise,
A gentle shimmer seen in your eyes.
Two hearts entwined, a dance so sweet,
The glow between us, a love discreet.

With every laugh, a spark ignites,
In shared moments, we reach new heights.
Together we shine, a radiant beam,
In the tapestry of life, we weave our dream.

## Radiance of Affection

Beneath the moon's watchful, tender gaze,
Your smile ignites a warm, golden blaze.
In every heartbeat, the world fades away,
The radiance of affection holds sway.

Through trials faced, we stand side by side,
In the depths of love, we take our stride.
With every touch, the universe glows,
In the warmth of your arms, the love grows.

# **A Beacon in the Night**

When darkness falls and shadows conspire,
You are the beacon that lifts me higher.
Guiding my spirit through the coldest night,
Your love, a lighthouse, shining so bright.

With every challenge, your light remains,
In storms of doubt, where fear reigns.
Together we stand, facing the strife,
A beacon in the night, you are my life.

## A Voyage to Illuminated Shores

Across the waves, a journey starts,
With dreams aglow, and hopeful hearts.
The stars above, a guide so bright,
Leading us forth into the night.

The winds whisper secrets of the sea,
Carrying wishes, wild and free.
With every tide, we dance and sway,
Embracing night, welcoming day.

Through storms we sail, we bend, we break,
But in the dawn, new paths we make.
The shores ahead, a promise sure,
A radiant light, forever pure.

With laughter echoing in the air,
We find our fortune, joys to share.
As lanterns flicker on the beach,
Our dreams awaken, within reach.

Together bound on this bright quest,
In every heart, our souls are blessed.
A voyage to shores where dreams reside,
Illuminated by love as our guide.

# Luminescence of Connection

In twilight's arms, we find our gleam,
Each glance exchanged, like woven dreams.
Our laughter shines, a brilliant light,
Illuminating the soft night.

Every word spoken, a gentle spark,
Kindled moments that leave their mark.
Through gentle touch, our spirits blend,
In this embrace, where hearts transcend.

A fusion bright, like stars aligned,
In the dance of fate, our souls entwined.
With whispers sweet, we paint the air,
Creating magic, a bond so rare.

As shadows fade, the dawn arises,
The glow of connection never disguises.
In every heartbeat, a rhythm shared,
A luminescence, unprepared.

Together we rise, like the sun anew,
In every endeavor, it's me and you.
A radiant path, where we will roam,
In the light of love, we find our home.

## The Glow of Yesterday

Through memories, we softly tread,
Recalling words that once were said.
Gentle echoes of laughter's song,
In the glow of yesterday, we belong.

Dances held beneath the stars,
Moments etched like timeless scars.
With every glance, our hearts entwined,
In the warmth of memories, love defined.

Fading photographs, a tender hue,
Each smile reflects what's ever true.
A golden light in shadows cast,
Reminds us of a cherished past.

In whispers soft, the tales arise,
Of dreams we chased, beneath the skies.
With every story, a flicker shines,
Illuminating all our designs.

The glow of yesterday stays near,
A guiding light, forever clear.
Through time we walk, hand in hand,
Carrying joy, like grains of sand.

# **Radiant Whispers**

In quiet corners, secrets dwell,
Whispers wrapped in a silken spell.
Subtle glimmers in twilight's gaze,
Shining softly through life's maze.

Like petals kissed by morning dew,
Each word spoken, ancient and new.
A gentle breeze, a lover's sigh,
Together we soar, oh how we fly.

Moments of silence, yet so profound,
In every heartbeat, love is found.
With tender glances, we weave the night,
In radiant whispers, everything feels right.

As stars unveil their dazzling light,
Stories unfold in the hush of night.
With every breath, our spirits dance,
In the quiet, we take our chance.

So let us linger in this embrace,
With whispered dreams that time can't erase.
In the warmth of these tender ties,
Radiant whispers will never die.

## **Heartbeats in Harmony**

In sync we move, a gentle dance,
Our laughter echoes, a sweet romance.
Each heartbeat sings a tune so pure,
In harmony's arms, we find our cure.

The world fades away, just us two,
Underneath the sky, deep and blue.
Every whisper, every sigh,
Ties our souls, like stars on high.

With every glance, our spirits soar,
Together in peace, forevermore.
In this embrace, time melts away,
Heartbeats in harmony, night and day.

## Together in Radiance

In the glow of friendship, we shine bright,
Guiding each other through darkest nights.
Hand in hand, we face the dawn,
Together in radiance, we are reborn.

With every smile, our spirits beam,
Chasing dreams like a vibrant stream.
Moments shared, a tapestry spun,
Together in radiance, we are one.

In laughter's warmth, in silent grace,
No distance can part, nor time erase.
Side by side, we laugh and play,
Together in radiance, come what may.

## The Brilliance of Shared Moments

In fleeting time, we find our bliss,
A stolen glance, a gentle kiss.
The world pauses, a perfect frame,
The brilliance of shared moments, our flame.

In laughter's ring, the joy ignites,
Every memory, our hearts' delights.
Through simple gestures, love unfolds,
The brilliance of shared moments, more precious than gold.

With every story, a bond we weave,
Treasure these times, we dare believe.
Together we stand, dreams in sight,
The brilliance of shared moments, our guiding light.

## **Beacons of Compassion**

In a world so vast, be the light,
Shining through shadows, chasing the night.
With open hearts, we reach and mend,
Beacons of compassion, love has no end.

A listening ear, a helping hand,
Together we rise, united we stand.
In small acts of kindness, we sow the seeds,
Beacons of compassion, fulfilling needs.

Through stormy days and sunny skies,
We'll lift each other, help dreams arise.
With strength in love, our spirits grow,
Beacons of compassion, let kindness flow.

## **The Light that Beckons**

A whisper in the still of night,
Stars twinkle like hope in flight.
Shadows fade, the dawn is near,
Follow the path, let go of fear.

With every step, warmth ignites,
Guiding us through endless sights.
Embrace the glow that leads the way,
In its embrace, we find our stay.

## **Heartfelt Illumination**

In the quiet, truth resides,
Illumination softly guides.
Words unspoken, yet they shine,
A connection so divine.

Beneath the surface, feelings rise,
A dance of hearts, with no disguise.
Every glance a heartfelt song,
In the light, we all belong.

**Reflections of Tenderness**

In mirrors bright, our souls reflect,
Tender moments we collect.
Gentle laughter, simple joys,
Embrace the warmth, the love deploys.

With open hearts, we share our dreams,
In the stillness, hope redeems.
Through every tear, a lesson learned,
In tender light, our spirits burned.

## The Dance of Light and Shade

A waltz of dusk, a graceful sway,
Light and shade in soft ballet.
Every flicker, every gleam,
Weaving stories, like a dream.

In twilight's embrace, shadows play,
Illuminating the lost array.
With every turn, we find our place,
In this dance, a warm embrace.

## Heartfelt Pathways

In quiet whispers, love resides,
Along the winding, gentle tides.
Each step we take, a bond we weave,
In heartfelt paths, we learn to believe.

The sun may set, the stars will glow,
With every heartbeat, feelings grow.
A tapestry of dreams unfolds,
In every story that love holds.

Through stormy nights and sunny days,
We walk together, in myriad ways.
The road may twist, but hand in hand,
We carve our future, a promised land.

From laughter shared to silent tears,
We cherish moments, through the years.
Every heartbeat sings a song,
In heartfelt pathways, we belong.

So let us wander, side by side,
No fear of where the path may tide.
With love as compass, we'll stay true,
In every step, I walk with you.

## **The Luminous Journey**

A whisper soft upon the night,
Guides us through shadows, into light.
With every turn, the heart ignites,
Embracing dreams, we chase the heights.

Through valleys deep, we find our way,
With hope as guide, we shall not sway.
United in this sweet embrace,
We seek the warmth of every place.

Stars above us shine so bright,
Guiding footsteps, pure delight.
With every breath, the world anew,
The luminous journey, me and you.

We dance through echoes of the past,
In fleeting moments, love holds fast.
Together weaving tales in the night,
A patchwork quilt of purest light.

So let the winds of fortune blow,
We'll face the tides, let courage grow.
For in each step, our story glows,
On this journey, love only knows.

## Embraces Beneath the Moon

Beneath the moon's soft, silver beams,
We share our laughter, hopes, and dreams.
The world around us fades away,
In every hug, the night holds sway.

Your warmth envelops, calm and true,
In tender moments, me and you.
With every sigh, the silence speaks,
Our hearts entwined, the joy it seeks.

The stars bear witness to our dance,
In whispered vows, we take a chance.
With every glance, a story spun,
Together we are, forever one.

As shadows stretch and daylight gleams,
We'll find our way through all extremes.
In love's embrace, our worries cease,
Beneath the moon, we find our peace.

So let the night wrap us in grace,
In this soft glow, we find our place.
With every heartbeat, side by side,
Embraces bloom like evening tide.

# **Threads of Celestial Light**

In swirling skies, our dreams ignite,
With threads of celestial light.
Each star a spark of hope divine,
In cosmic patterns, love will shine.

We weave our tales in skies above,
With every thread, we craft our love.
Through galaxies, our spirits soar,
In every moment, we explore.

The universe sings a symphony,
Guided by fate, it's you and me.
With every heartbeat, a story spun,
Threads of connection, two become one.

So let the stars bear witness true,
To all the magic that we do.
In boundless spaces, our spirits unite,
In threads of celestial light.

Forever woven in this dance,
In every glance, we find our chance.
In endless wonder, hearts take flight,
As we embrace the cosmic night.

## The Warmth of Your Presence

In the gentle glow of your smile,
I find my heart's embrace,
Every moment feels worthwhile,
You bring me to a safer place.

With quiet laughter in the air,
You chase the shadows far away,
A tender touch, a loving care,
In your warmth, I long to stay.

The world outside may chill and freeze,
But in your arms, I feel the heat,
Your presence whispers, brings me ease,
A secret place, where souls can meet.

As we share dreams beneath the night,
Each heartbeat echoes vibrant sound,
Together, we create the light,
In your warmth, my joy is found.

Forever wrapped in love's embrace,
I cherish each soft, fleeting glance,
In the warmth of your sacred space,
Life dances on, a tender dance.

## Guiding Stars of Tenderness

In the quiet sky, they gleam,
Soft whispers of the night,
Guiding us like a fleeting dream,
Stars shining ever bright.

Each glowing orb tells a tale,
Of love that spans the years,
Through every joy and every pale,
They watch and dry our tears.

When loneliness begins to creep,
These stars will light our way,
In every promise we do keep,
They guide us, come what may.

With every wish cast to the sky,
Tenderness holds us near,
In their glow, we learn to fly,
Embracing love, not fear.

So let us dance beneath their gaze,
With hearts that beat in tune,
Guided by their gentle blaze,
We'll look up to the moon.

## **Brilliance of Belonging**

In the laughter shared, we find,
A tapestry so bright,
Woven threads of heart and mind,
Together, we ignite.

Each moment holds a memory,
A spark that lights the dark,
Through trials, we gain clarity,
Together, we leave a mark.

In the depths of every trial,
We strengthen, hand in hand,
With every challenge, every mile,
Our bond, forever grand.

The brilliance of our souls aligned,
Creates a vibrant hue,
In the warmth of love, we're intertwined,
With skies of endless blue.

So let us cherish every sign,
The beauty of our song,
For in this life, your heart is mine,
Where all of us belong.

# Lanterns of Connection

In the shadowed paths we roam,
You hold a light so clear,
With every step, we feel at home,
Finding solace near.

These lanterns flicker in the night,
Illuminating the way,
With every warmth, we share our light,
Chasing our fears away.

From heart to heart, the glow expands,
A bridge across the dark,
Together we can make great plans,
Fueling every spark.

In the moments that we share,
Connection is the key,
With every glance, a soft repair,
Uniting you and me.

So let us carry on this quest,
With lanterns held up high,
In the realms of love, we're truly blessed,
Beneath the endless sky.

## The Embrace of Dawn

In the stillness of night,
Dreams dance in soft flight.
A whisper of light breaks,
Awakening the lakes.

Gentle hues start to blend,
As shadows begin to bend.
The sun's kiss on the face,
Bringing in warmth and grace.

Chirping birds serenade,
In the dawn's cool cascade.
Morning dew glistens bright,
A canvas of pure light.

The world yawns and stirs,
As the soft breeze occurs.
Nature's melody swells,
With untold stories it tells.

Embracing the new day,
Let worries slip away.
With every breath we take,
The dawn's love we embrace.

## **Twinkling Hearts**

In the quiet of the night,
Stars scatter, pure and bright.
Hearts twinkle like the skies,
In a dance where hope lies.

Laughter echoes through time,
In moments so sublime.
Each spark a memory made,
In our secret parades.

Hand in hand, we roam free,
Woven like a tapestry.
In every whispered dream,
Our souls begin to gleam.

Through the shadows we glide,
With love as our guide.
Every heartbeat a song,
In a world where we belong.

As the universe spins,
A journey where love wins.
Twinkling hearts aligned,
In the night, forever kind.

## **Glowing Embers of Trust**

In the hearth of our bond,
Glowing sparks, we respond.
Each gesture, soft and warm,
In the night, a calming charm.

Trust builds like a flame,
Flickering, never the same.
Nurtured by gentle care,
In the silence, we share.

Through trials and the pain,
In the rain, joy remains.
Embers whisper our fate,
As we patiently wait.

Together we stand strong,
In each other, we belong.
Trust glows in eyes so bright,
Guiding us through the night.

With every breath, we ignite,
A bond that feels so right.
Glowing embers of trust,
A sacred bond, a must.

## Sparks of Serenity

In the hush of twilight's glow,
Peaceful waters gently flow.
Sparks of joy in the air,
A moment free of care.

Whispers of the gentle breeze,
Carry secrets through the trees.
Calmness settles like the dew,
As dreams begin anew.

Stars appear, a tranquil sight,
Guiding us into the night.
Each spark a piece of grace,
Illuminating our space.

Moments linger, soft and still,
Filling hearts with a thrill.
In the silence, we find delight,
Sparks of serenity ignite.

As we breathe in the night,
Feeling the world alight.
In this harmony we stay,
Lost in peace, come what may.

## Embrace the Brilliance

In the dawn's soft glow, we rise,
Hearts ignited, dreams in our eyes.
With each breath, we soar and dive,
In this moment, we come alive.

Among the stars, the night unfolds,
Stories of courage, yet untold.
With every step, we leave our mark,
Guided by hope, igniting the spark.

Through the shadows, we find our way,
Together we shine, come what may.
Hand in hand, we face our fears,
Embracing life, through laughter and tears.

In the tapestry of love, we weave,
A world of wonder, we'll believe.
The brilliance within us, forever bright,
Together we'll light up the night.

So dance with joy, let spirits fly,
In the brilliance, we touch the sky.
With open hearts, we take a chance,
Embracing life, we join the dance.

# **Shimmering Threads of Connection**

In the quiet, a whisper grows,
Through tangled paths, our spirit flows.
Each heart a thread, vibrant and bold,
Together we weave a tale untold.

With every glance, a bond ignites,
In the darkness, we find our lights.
A tapestry rich, with love's embrace,
In every stitch, we find our place.

Through laughter shared and tears that fall,
The shimmering threads connect us all.
In every touch, a spark of grace,
In this dance of life, we find our space.

From distant shores, our echoes ring,
In moments fleeting, we gather, we sing.
A symphony woven, in harmony bound,
In this sacred circle, love is found.

So let us cherish these moments dear,
In the shimmering glow, we persevere.
With open hearts, let connections grow,
In the fabric of life, our spirits flow.

## Celestial Whisper

In the stillness of the night sky,
Stars are secrets, waiting to fly.
A celestial hush, the world at peace,
In these moments, worries cease.

Softly the moon spills silver light,
Guiding dreamers through the night.
Each twinkle tells a tale of old,
Of wishes made and hearts consoled.

In every shadow, a glimpse of hope,
Through cosmic pathways, we learn to cope.
With every heartbeat, a universe spins,
In the silence, the magic begins.

Let the stars cradle your dreams tight,
As the dawn approaches, chasing the night.
Whispers of wonder fill the air,
In the embrace of the cosmos, we dare.

So breathe in deep, let your spirit soar,
In the celestial dance, there's always more.
With every wish, let your heart take flight,
Under the veil of the endless night.

**Radiant Journeys**

With every step on this radiant road,
We carry the dreams that spark and glowed.
Through valleys low and mountains high,
Onward we wander, reaching the sky.

In the laughter shared and the tears we shed,
Each moment a story, patiently spread.
With courage as our guiding light,
We embrace the unknown, fueled by insight.

The paths we travel are steep and wide,
But together, we walk with hearts open wide.
In the embrace of friendship, we find our way,
Through the darkest nights to the brightest day.

With hearts ablaze, we venture forth,
Chasing the sun as the stars give birth.
Every journey leads to new beginnings,
In the dance of life, we find our winnings.

So let the radiant dreams take flight,
Through shadows and storms, we shine bright.
In this beautiful dance, we'll find our true plea,
Together forever, just you and me.

## **The Light That Connects**

In shadows deep, there lies a spark,
A gentle glow that warms the dark.
It threads through hearts, a silver line,
Binding us close, your soul to mine.

A beacon bright, it calls us near,
With every whisper, soft and clear.
Through stormy nights and endless day,
This light will guide us on our way.

Across the miles, it shines so true,
A lighthouse bright, it leads me to you.
In every glance, in every sigh,
This radiant bond will never die.

Together we stand, fearless and bold,
Our stories woven, forever told.
Through trials faced, we'll never part,
This light, a flame that warms the heart.

# **Echoes of Devotion**

In every heartbeat, love resounds,
A melody in silence found.
Whispers dance in tender air,
In echoes sweet, we find our care.

Through the years, our vows remain,
A soft refrain, through joy and pain.
In laughter's warmth and sorrow's grace,
Our spirits meet in this sacred space.

Beneath the stars, where dreams take flight,
We share our hopes in the still of night.
With every promise, pure and deep,
In echoes of devotion, our love we keep.

Let time unfold, let moments flow,
In every beat, our spirits glow.
Together strong, we'll stand as one,
In echoes of love, our journey's spun.

## **Celestial Affection**

Beneath the vast and starry sky,
Our hearts align, as comets fly.
In lunar light, we chase our dreams,
Through night's embrace, love softly gleams.

Galaxies swirl in your embrace,
In every touch, a gentle grace.
With every pulse, the cosmos hums,
In this dance, eternity comes.

Constellations tell our tale,
In cosmic winds, we set our sail.
Through storms and calm, our spirits soar,
Together bound, forevermore.

Celestial bodies, intertwined,
In every heartbeat, love defined.
With every breath, our souls ignite,
In celestial affection, pure delight.

# **Shimmering Souls**

In a world of shadows and light,
Shimmering souls take to flight.
With every spark, a story told,
In vibrant hues, our dreams unfold.

Through whispered winds and gentle streams,
We chase the echo of our dreams.
With every glance, a universe,
In shimmering souls, we find our verse.

Together we weave a tapestry,
Of love and hope, eternally free.
In radiant hues, our spirits glow,
In this luminous dance, we overflow.

With every dawn, new colors bloom,
In shimmering souls, dispelling gloom.
Hand in hand, we'll face the day,
In radiant love, we'll find our way.

## Starlit Promises

Underneath the wide, dark sky,
Whispers of hope, they softly sigh.
Stars like diamonds, bright and clear,
Holding secrets we long to hear.

Memories dance in silver light,
Guiding hearts through the velvet night.
Promises made with every glance,
Dreams awaken in a cosmic trance.

Moments frozen, time stands still,
With every heartbeat, a quiet thrill.
In the stillness, we find our way,
Chasing shadows till break of day.

Together we stand, hand in hand,
As the universe makes its stand.
Every wish upon a star,
Brings us closer, no matter how far.

In starlit nights, our stories weave,
Infinite tales of love and believe.
Each twinkle holds a promise true,
Forever bound, just me and you.

## **Illuminated Reveries**

In dreams we drift on clouds of light,
Chasing visions through the night.
Colors blend in soft embrace,
We paint the canvas of this space.

Gentle echoes softly glide,
Navigating the moments wide.
Thoughts take flight, like birds in air,
Freedom found in dreams we share.

Eager hearts, they intertwine,
Laughter ringing, divine sign.
In the glow of this serene place,
Magic dances with every trace.

Quiet whispers fill the void,
In each sigh, our fears destroyed.
Illuminated paths we roam,
In this wonder, we find home.

With every heartbeat, a story told,
In radiant hues, dreams unfold.
Together we weave our reverie,
In this light, forever free.

## Dances in the Glow

Twilight wraps us in its embrace,
Shadows flicker, leaving no trace.
Footsteps gentle on the ground,
In the warmth, our hearts are found.

With every heartbeat, we align,
In soft whispers, your hand in mine.
Around us swirls a golden haze,
In this moment, we drift and gaze.

Stars above join in our dance,
A symphony of sweet romance.
As time dissolves, we lose control,
Every move ignites the soul.

In the rhythm, we find our way,
Floating freely, come what may.
Underneath the watchful sky,
In the glow, our spirits fly.

With every twirl, we leave behind,
The worries of the daily grind.
Moments cherished, hearts aglow,
Together forever, in the flow.

# A Radiant Connection

In the stillness, our hearts beat,
Drawing closer, a warmth so sweet.
Electric pulses through the air,
In this moment, nothing else compares.

Eyes meet like stars in the night,
Illuminated by love's pure light.
Every glance holds a thousand words,
Unspoken dreams, like soaring birds.

Together, we weave a tender spell,
In silent whispers, our stories swell.
Hands entwined, we walk this path,
Embracing joy, escaping wrath.

Connections forged in timeless space,
As we dance at a gentle pace.
Unraveled hopes like waves unfurled,
In our universe, love is swirled.

As radiant souls, we glow with grace,
In this dance, we find our place.
With every heartbeat, dreams align,
In this connection, forever divine.

## **Celestial Embrace**

Beneath the stars we find our place,
Whispers of the night, a gentle grace.
In the cosmos, our spirits dance,
Lost in the magic of this chance.

Moonlit shadows cast a spell,
Tales of love, we weave so well.
Hands entwined, hearts intertwined,
In this moment, forever aligned.

Shooting stars that cross the sky,
Each one promising, a silent sigh.
In their glow, we find our dream,
Celestial paths, a timeless beam.

Galaxies pulse with each heartbeat,
Together, we rise, never to retreat.
The universe wrapped us tight,
In this embrace, all feels right.

In the distance, planets hum,
To the rhythm of love, we've become.
Journeying through the cosmos so wide,
In celestial embrace, we gently glide.

## **The Light We Share**

In the dawn, a beacon bright,
Guiding souls through the night.
Each shimmer holds a hidden care,
A promise found in the light we share.

Flickers dance upon the sea,
Echoing whispers, wild and free.
In the warmth of sunlit skies,
Our joy and laughter always rise.

Moments weave like threads of gold,
Stories of love, eternally told.
In every heartbeat, in every glance,
The light we share is our true romance.

Stars above us, bright and clear,
Illuminate dreams that linger near.
Together, we'll chase the shadows away,
Creating memories that forever stay.

As dusk falls, we won't despair,
In the glow of love, we found our layer.
Through each trial, we will declare,
Forever strong, in the light we share.

## **Flickers of Togetherness**

In twilight's glow, we find our spark,
Amidst the whispers, together embark.
Flickers cast in gentle hues,
Moments cherished, hearts we choose.

Like fireflies in a summer's night,
We dance and sway, with pure delight.
Each laugh a note, each sigh a song,
In this symphony, we both belong.

Through winding paths, hand in hand,
In the chaos, we'll always stand.
Each flicker tells a story true,
Of love enduring, forever anew.

In the quiet, in the loud,
Together, we rise, we break the crowd.
With every glance, we reaffirm,
In this togetherness, we truly learn.

A tapestry of shared embrace,
Woven together, a sacred space.
As shadows blend and daylight fades,
In flickers of togetherness, hope cascades.

## Kindred Brightness

In the depths of the midnight sky,
Our spirits twinkle, soaring high.
Bound by love, a radiant thread,
Kindred souls, where dreams are spread.

Beneath the glow, we make our way,
Through silent woods, where nightbirds play.
Each whispered secret fuels the fire,
Kindred brightness, our hearts aspire.

With every dawn, new colors bloom,
Erasing shadows, chasing gloom.
In each sunrise, a tale unfolds,
Of kindred spirits, brave and bold.

We journey forth, side by side,
In this adventure, we boldly glide.
Wherever we roam, we'll share the light,
In kindred brightness, we take flight.

As twilight calls, we'll dance anew,
In the embrace of stars, just us two.
Forever guided by fate's sweet kiss,
In kindred brightness, we find our bliss.

## **Warmth in the Shadows**

In twilight's hush, we find our peace,
A gentle whisper, a soft release.
With every breath, the night unfolds,
Embracing secrets that time beholds.

Stars above, like fireflies bright,
Guide us gently through the night.
In the shadows, our laughter sings,
A dance of warmth that love brings.

Fingers entwined, we brave the dark,
In silent spaces, we leave a mark.
Together we cradle the fleeting hour,
In the shadows, we bloom like a flower.

The moon casts light on dreams we share,
Crafted moments, tender and rare.
In quiet corners, our hopes ignite,
Filling shadows with soft, golden light.

Through whispered winds, we find our way,
Turning doubts into a bright display.
For in the shadow, we craft our song,
Where love whispers, we are strong.

# **Heartfelt Compass**

In every heartbeat, a path is drawn,
A compass governed by the dawn.
With every step, we seek to find,
The treasures held within the mind.

Through mountains high and valleys low,
We chart the course of love's bright glow.
A guiding star in skies so vast,
Our heartfelt compass, steadfast.

With gentle words and tender grace,
We traverse life, an endless chase.
In every glance, a promise made,
In storms and sunshine, we won't fade.

The journey leads to places new,
With hands held tight, and skies so blue.
Navigating by the heart's own light,
Through shadows deep, we find our sight.

In quiet moments, we pause to dream,
A world of hope, a radiant beam.
With every heartbeat, our dreams take flight,
Together always, we find our might.

## The Glow of Togetherness

In the stillness of evening's grace,
We find the warmth of a familiar space.
With laughter weaving through the air,
The glow of togetherness found everywhere.

Shared glances spark like distant stars,
Radiating light, no matter the scars.
In cozy corners, our spirits rise,
In the heart's embrace, love never lies.

Through seasons change and time's swift flow,
The bonds we forge, only we know.
Hand in hand, through thick and thin,
The glow of togetherness draws us in.

In stories told by fire's light,
We gather close, hearts shining bright.
With every moment, our roots run deep,
In unity's warmth, our souls will leap.

Together we dance, the world fades away,
In this glow, forever we stay.
A sanctuary found, where love is real,
In the glow of togetherness, we heal.

## A Flicker in the Dark

In the depths of night, a flicker appears,
A beacon of hope in the sea of fears.
With every spark, the shadows relent,
Guiding our hearts where the light is sent.

Whispers echo in silence profound,
In this stillness, new dreams abound.
We chase the glimmers, we follow the light,
Finding our way through the endless night.

A candle's flame sways soft and low,
Casting warmth in the dark's quiet flow.
In each gentle flicker, a story unfolds,
Of courage, love, and dreams retold.

Through trials faced and shadows cast,
A flicker remains, steadfast and vast.
In the heart of the storm, we find our way,
With hope's tiny flicker, we seize the day.

Together we rise, hand in hand,
Illuminated paths, forever we stand.
For in unity's light, our spirits embark,
On a journey of love—a flicker in the dark.

## Radiance of the Heart

In the morning's light, we rise,
With whispers soft, the spirit sighs.
A bloom of warmth, a gentle spark,
Love's sweet song ignites the dark.

With every beat, a dance begins,
A tapestry where hope still spins.
Layers of joy, enkindled bright,
Guiding us through the silent night.

Each glance a flame, each touch pure gold,
In the embrace, our stories told.
Together we paint the canvas vast,
Holding tight to the shadows cast.

Through trials faced and rivers crossed,
We find the love that never lost.
In moments fleeting, we'll remain,
The radiance that wipes the pain.

In every heartbeat, every sigh,
Our spirits soar, like birds we fly.
In harmony, our souls align,
In the radiance, forever shine.

## **Illuminate My Soul**

In twilight's hue, where dreams take flight,
I seek the spark, the guiding light.
With open arms, let shadows fade,
Illuminate my soul, unafraid.

The stars above begin to weave,
A tapestry of hope, believe.
With every word, my heart unwinds,
In your aura, solace finds.

Let not the dark cloud heavy fall,
For in your glow, I feel the call.
A whisper soft, the night invites,
Illuminate my soul, through darkest nights.

With every glance, a silent tune,
A dance beneath the silver moon.
Your light, a beacon, leading me,
To realms of pure serenity.

Each cherished moment, bright and clear,
With every heartbeat, I draw near.
In your embrace, I lose control,
Forever cherished, my soul whole.

## Beacon of Embrace

In the stillness of the night,
Your warmth surrounds, a gentle light.
A beacon shines through shadows deep,
In your embrace, my heart will leap.

Through troubled waters, we will sail,
In unity, we shall prevail.
With whispered dreams, together grow,
A love that's deep, a steady flow.

With every laugh, a spark ignites,
Guiding us through the endless nights.
Your arms, a harbor, safe and strong,
Where we belong, where hearts belong.

The path we tread, with hands entwined,
In fondness pure, our souls aligned.
Your essence glows, a guiding star,
A beacon bright, no matter how far.

In every challenge, in every tear,
We find the strength, the love sincere.
With every heartbeat, keep the pace,
Forever bound in our warm embrace.

## **Luminescent Affection**

Beneath the moon's tender gaze,
Our hearts dance in a timeless daze.
In every whisper of the night,
A luminescent glow, pure delight.

With loving words, the air is sweet,
In your presence, all feels complete.
Together we navigate the tide,
In luminescent affection, we confide.

Through every trial, we find our way,
With gentle hearts, we choose to stay.
A bond that brightens every day,
In sweet affection, come what may.

The world may change, the seasons turn,
But in our hearts, a fire will burn.
With every glance, a promise made,
In luminescent love, never fade.

As stars collide and shadows play,
In your embrace, I long to stay.
With every heartbeat, I adore,
A luminescent love, forevermore.

## **Heartstrings in Twilight**

In the hush of twilight's grace,
Whispers soft as dreams embrace.
Stars awaken, skies unite,
Love ignites the fading light.

Moments linger, hearts entwined,
In the glow, our souls aligned.
Echoes of a sweet refrain,
Dance like shadows, joy and pain.

Every breath, a gentle sigh,
As the day begins to die.
Fingers trace the starlit sky,
Together here, you and I.

Colors blend, the night unfolds,
In silence, stories to be told.
In twilight's calm, we find our way,
Heartstrings bind, come what may.

Underneath the fading sun,
Our journey's just begun.
A tapestry of dreams we weave,
In this moment, we believe.

## The Warmth of Togetherness

In a world that often chills,
Love's embrace, our hearts it fills.
Through the storms, we hold so tight,
Finding strength in shared delight.

Laughter dances in the air,
In your gaze, I feel your care.
Every step, a shared delight,
Together, we create our light.

Cup of warmth in winter's frost,
In your arms, I never feel lost.
Stories shared beside the flame,
In togetherness, we'll never be the same.

Through the shadows, we will roam,
In your heart, I've found my home.
Hand in hand, we'll face the night,
In our circle, purest light.

With your laughter, joy returns,
In your presence, my heart yearns.
Every moment feels like gold,
In our togetherness, love unfolds.

## Luminous Bonds

Like stars that twinkle in the night,
Our connection feels so bright.
Radiant threads that intertwine,
A luminous love that feels divine.

Through the dark, you are my guide,
In your warmth, I safely bide.
Every laugh, a spark that glows,
Guiding paths where love still grows.

With every heartbeat, we ignite,
A bond that dances, pure delight.
In the glow of our embrace,
Time stands still, a sacred space.

Together we paint the skies,
With colors drawn from our sighs.
In the tapestry of our days,
Luminous bonds light our ways.

Through the storms, we'll shine so bright,
In our souls, eternal light.
Hand in hand, we'll always find,
Luminous love, forever kind.

## Serenity's Embrace

In a meadow, soft and warm,
Peace envelops, free from harm.
Gentle breezes kiss the grass,
In serenity, moments pass.

Whispers of the trees above,
Nature's song, a hymn of love.
Sunbeams dance, a golden glow,
In this haven, worries go.

Every sigh, a breath of peace,
In this stillness, sweet release.
With open hearts, we find our way,
To a dawn that greets the day.

Together, we will sit awhile,
Share our dreams, ignite a smile.
In the quiet, time suspends,
In serenity, our love transcends.

As the stars begin to peek,
In this bliss, we softly speak.
Wrapped in calm, we feel the grace,
Of love and peace in space.

## Celestial Poetry

Stars above in velvet night,
Whispers soft, a pure delight.
Galaxies dance in cosmic flow,
Eternal tales they weave and sow.

Wishes carried on the breeze,
Moonlit paths, the heart's unease.
Constellations, dreams made bright,
In the silence, find your light.

Rivers of time, they twist and turn,
Lessons of love, we slowly learn.
Each heartbeat echoes, soft and clear,
In this poetry, hold me near.

Voices rise, a gentle hum,
In this vastness, we become.
Together, always intertwined,
In celestial dreams, love defined.

So gaze upon the endless night,
Let stars guide us, pure delight.
In the cosmos, hand in hand,
Our hearts united, ever planned.

## Illuminated Pathways of Togetherness

Through fields of gold, our laughter flows,
Hand in hand, as soft winds blow.
Each step we take lights up the path,
Bringing joy, escaping wrath.

Moments shared in sunlit glow,
Where love blooms and rivers flow.
Bonded souls with stories told,
In this journey, brave and bold.

Stars align on the road we tread,
Every word, like silk, is spread.
In your eyes, the world I see,
Illuminated, you and me.

Echoes of laughter fill the air,
With every glance, a gentle care.
As shadows dance, we brave the night,
Together, we'll always find the light.

In these moments, time stands still,
Hearts entwined with steadfast will.
Forever woven, paths we share,
In togetherness, we find our flare.

# Shining Moments of Forever

In twilight's glow, our dreams ignite,
Moments captured, pure delight.
Hand in hand, we face the dawn,
In your warmth, I feel reborn.

Time may shift like whispering trees,
Yet in your eyes, my spirit sees.
With every heartbeat, echoes play,
In shining moments, we find our way.

The universe, a canvas wide,
With colors bold and hearts as guide.
Through stormy nights and sunny days,
Together, love forever stays.

Laughter rings like chimes of hope,
In each challenge, we learn to cope.
Past the valleys, towards the peaks,
In every longing, love speaks.

So let us dance through endless time,
With every step, our hearts in rhyme.
Shining moments, yours and mine,
In forever's grasp, love will shine.

## **Whispers of the Heart**

In the quiet, whispers flow,
Secrets only we can know.
Gentle sighs and tender dreams,
The heart knows more than it seems.

Through shadows deep, we navigate,
With love, we choose to celebrate.
Every heartbeat, a story shared,
In whispers soft, we're unprepared.

In the stillness, hope takes flight,
Guiding us through darkest night.
Together, we will always stand,
In softly spoken, crafted plans.

Dancing close, we feel the spark,
Illuminating every dark.
In your gaze, my soul can soar,
With every whisper, I want more.

In the quiet, let love dwell,
With whispers that we know so well.
Hearts united, never apart,
In the stillness, our love's art.

## Light in the Lovelorn Night

In shadows deep where whispers roam,
A flicker shines, a heart's soft home.
Amidst the gloom of sorrow's flight,
Hope's gentle glow lights up the night.

With every tear, a star is born,
Each sigh a wish, a love reborn.
In dreams we chase, in silence fight,
We find our way in lovelorn light.

Through empty streets where echoes play,
The warmth of love, it finds a way.
In fleeting moments, pure delight,
We hold our breath, embrace the night.

The moon above, a guardian bright,
Bears witness to our hearts' insight.
Together, bound, in tender white,
We dance beneath the lovelorn night.

So let us weave, through pain and grace,
A tapestry in this sacred space.
For every heart that yearns for right,
There shines a light in lovelorn night.

## The Hearth of Unity

In the center of our gathering place,
Where laughter thrives and hearts embrace.
The flames of friendship warm the air,
A beacon bright, a bond so rare.

With stories shared and moments blessed,
We find our peace, our souls at rest.
Each voice a note in harmony,
Together we build our unity.

In trials faced, we stand as one,
The journey shared, the race we've run.
A circle strong, with love ignited,
By the hearth of unity, united.

Embrace the fire that never fades,
Our spirits lift, our hope cascades.
In every heart, a flame so true,
The warmth of us, a vibrant hue.

So gather here, in joy and trust,
For in each other, we find our must.
Together we rise, our fears outdone,
In the hearth of unity, we are one.

## Sunbeam of Tenderness

A gentle touch upon the skin,
A whisper soft, where love begins.
In every smile, a sunbeam gleams,
Awakening the purest dreams.

The world may shift, the shadows creep,
But in your arms, my heart will leap.
A warmth that chases all my fears,
Your love, a balm for all my tears.

In twilight's glow, we dance so near,
Each heartbeat sings, your voice I hear.
A melody of sweet caress,
A sunbeam casts its tenderness.

Through every storm, your light remains,
A guiding star through joys and pains.
With every glance, my soul you bless,
Enwrapped in warmth, in tenderness.

So let us bask in love's embrace,
Together, here, in time and space.
For in your eyes, the world is clear,
A sunbeam bright, forever dear.

## Navigating with Lumens

In darkest night, we chart our course,
With glowing hearts, we find our source.
Each step we take, a path we write,
Navigating through the starry light.

With every beam, a story speaks,
Of hopes and dreams, in silent peaks.
Through trials faced, we shine so bright,
Together we sail, our futures bright.

The lanterns glow, our spirits bold,
With every tale, a truth retold.
In unity, we rise from fright,
Navigating calmly with lumens bright.

Through uncharted seas, we find our way,
With laughter's song, we greet the day.
Each moment shared, a pure delight,
Our hearts united in the light.

So let us roam, through night and day,
With luminous dreams to light the way.
For every heart that takes to flight,
Finds solace in navigating with lumens.

## **Tides of Affection**

In the quiet whisper of the night,
Waves of love dance in soft moonlight.
Gentle breezes carry sweet sighs,
As the ocean of heart never lies.

Moments ebb and flow like the sea,
Each touch ignites a sweet plea.
With every tide, our spirits blend,
Woven together, we transcend.

Through storms that rage and winds that howl,
In each other's arms, we find our prowl.
Guided by the stars above,
Navigating the depths of our love.

Seashells hold secrets, stories untold,
In the warmth of your gaze, I behold.
Anchored in trust, we drift and sway,
Our hearts forever on a vast bay.

With each sunset painting the sky,
We embrace the dusk, we never say goodbye.
As the tides of affection gently rise,
In your love, my spirit flies.

**Illuminated Memories**

Flickering candles in the dark,
Each flame whispers a cherished spark.
Beneath the stars, our laughter glows,
In every moment, our love grows.

Fragments of time softly woven,
In the heart's fabric, deeply frozen.
Echoes of joy, bittersweet tunes,
Dance in the shadows, beneath the moon.

Photos fading, yet feelings stay,
In the gallery of yesterday.
Brushstrokes of dreams upon the mind,
Illuminated paths we find.

Each heartbeat rings a familiar bell,
In stories we share, we dwell.
Time may scatter, but love remains,
Through the laughter, through the pains.

Together we build a timeless frame,
Crafting warmth from each unique flame.
Illuminated memories we hold dear,
Forever cherished, year after year.

## **The Brilliance of You**

In the dawn's embrace, your light appears,
Chasing away shadows, calming my fears.
Every smile shines like a star,
Illuminating the distance, near or far.

With your laughter, the world ignites,
Painting my days in vibrant sights.
Colors bloom where your presence lies,
In the brilliance of you, my spirit flies.

Through life's journey, hand in hand,
Together we traverse, we understand.
In the quiet moments, love's pure glow,
Each heartbeat sings, a rhythmic flow.

You are the poem I've always sought,
In every letter, in every thought.
With every glance, a spark ignites,
Reminding me of love's delights.

The brilliance of you lights my way,
Turning ordinary into a ballet.
A shining beacon, forever true,
In this vast world, it's just me and you.

## **Heartfelt Navigations**

In the maze of life, we find our way,
With heartfelt maps, we gently sway.
Every path leads to dreams we chase,
In trust's embrace, we find our place.

With compass hearts, we steer through storms,
Navigating love in all its forms.
Charting new courses with each embrace,
Together, we dance in this sacred space.

Each turn taken, a lesson learned,
In the fire of passion, our hearts burned.
Through valleys deep and mountains high,
We soar through the clouds, together we fly.

In the silence of night, whispers guide,
Promises held with unwavering pride.
Every heartbeat a rhythm we share,
In heartfelt navigations, we declare.

So here we stand, with dreams in hand,
On this journey, forever we'll stand.
Through every twist, our love's the anchor,
In heartfelt navigations, we'll never falter.

# Celestial Bonds

Under a blanket of shimmering stars,
We soar through realms, free as we dream.
Time dances lightly, without any bars,
In the cosmos, we're forever a team.

Galaxies whisper secrets of old,
Our laughter echoes through celestial tracks.
Together we traverse, bold and untold,
In the endless night, there's nothing we lack.

Every comet's tail ignites our spark,
Lighting the way through the vast divine.
In the shadow of planets, we leave our mark,
And trace the patterns where fates entwine.

Heartbeats sync with the pulse of the night,
In constellations, our love shines bright.
Through gravity's pull, and endless flight,
Together we dance in the soft starlight.

Beneath the moon's watchful gaze, we rest,
In the cradle of dreams, our souls align.
With celestial bonds, we are truly blessed,
In the universe's embrace, your hand in mine.

## Candlelight Conversations

In the glow of whispers, shadows play,
Softly we share our secrets and fears.
Candlelight flickers, dancing away,
Illuminating hearts, calming our tears.

Each word is a flame, tender and warm,
Drawing us closer, lost in the night.
In this soft solace, we weather the storm,
Finding our solace in flickering light.

Moments are timeless, each glance a thread,
Stitched with the gold of our shared delight.
With every flame, a memory is fed,
In candlelight's glow, the world feels right.

Laughter and sighs blend into one sound,
Softened by wax, time gently unfurls.
Together we sit, our hearts tightly bound,
Weaving wild dreams in a dance of whirls.

As the candles wane, the night wears thin,
Yet the warmth lingers, a sweet aftertaste.
In the light of our conversation, we win,
Creating forever in shadows embraced.

## A Light that Endures

In the depths of darkness, a spark ignites,
A flicker of hope that refuses to fade.
Through trials and shadows, it bravely fights,
This light within us, a promise conveyed.

Through storms of despair, it finds its way,
Guiding our footsteps with warmth and grace.
In moments of doubt, it will always stay,
A beacon of love in the coldest place.

With every heartbeat, this flame rises high,
A tapestry woven with threads of trust.
Even when time tries to pass by,
Together we shine; it's always a must.

As the world shifts, and seasons do turn,
This light, it endures through every change.
In its soft glow, we forever learn,
That what we hold dear can never exchange.

So hold this light close, let it lead your way,
For in its warm glow, together we'll soar.
With hearts intertwined, come what may,
This light that endures will forever endure.

## **Radiating Affection**

With every heartbeat, love's warmth expands,
Like sunlight spilling through a morning haze.
In the simple moments, we take our stands,
Radiating affection in countless ways.

Each smile a spark, igniting the air,
A touch that lingers, tender and sweet.
In soft embrace, we banish despair,
Creating our haven where souls may meet.

Your laughter resonates, a melody pure,
In harmony, we dance through life's sweet game.
Together we find a love that's secure,
In every heartbeat, we're never the same.

Through trials and triumphs, our love will shine,
A beacon of strength through the trials we face.
In radiance found, our spirits align,
With affection that time cannot erase.

So let us cherish each moment, each sigh,
For in our connection, the world feels right.
Together forever, just you and I,
Radiating affection, a beautiful light.

## The Brightness of Us

In the dawn of day, we rise,
With laughter echoing in the skies.
Hand in hand, we walk this space,
Together, we find our place.

The sun spills gold on our skin,
Filling our hearts, warming within.
Every glance a spark of light,
Guiding us through day and night.

With every smile, we ignite,
A fire that makes the shadows bright.
In your eyes, I see the glow,
A universe only we know.

Through the storms and the rain,
We hold each other through the pain.
In the darkest of our plight,
Love's brightness becomes our sight.

Together, we shine and gleam,
Reality blending with a dream.
In our world, forever we trust,
For nothing compares to the brightness of us.

## **Illuminated Dreams**

In the stillness of the night,
We chase the stars, burning bright.
Each dream a whisper of the heart,
Guiding us, a work of art.

Through the shadows yet untold,
With hopes and wishes, we are bold.
Every thought a lantern raised,
In the dark, we are amazed.

Time dances softly, swift and free,
In the silence, just you and me.
With every sigh, our dreams expand,
Illuminated by love's hand.

Fleeting moments softly gleam,
Awakening the sweetest dream.
Eternal echoes fill the space,
As we lose ourselves in grace.

Floating on a night so deep,
With memories that we will keep.
In the light of our delight,
We weave our dreams, shining bright.

## **A Journey of Tender Hearts**

With gentle steps, we start this quest,
Two tender souls, forever blessed.
Each heartbeat a promise, pure and true,
In this journey, it's me and you.

From mountain highs to valleys low,
A tapestry of love we sew.
Through winding paths, we learn and grow,
In the warmth of our hearts, we glow.

Life's challenges may come and sway,
Together, we'll find our way.
Hand in hand, through thick and thin,
With every loss, there's love to win.

In soft whispers, we share our dreams,
Each moment bursting at the seams.
Every memory a work of art,
Sealed forever in tender hearts.

Through laughter shared and tears that fall,
We rise again, we stand tall.
In this journey, we will find,
The love that lingers, unconfined.

## The Compass of Our Souls

Beneath the stars, our paths align,
With every heartbeat, your hand in mine.
The compass sways to love's embrace,
In the journey, we find our place.

Through forests vast and rivers wide,
In every moment, you are my guide.
Trusting the signs that fate imparts,
Together we navigate our hearts.

When shadows loom and fears arise,
Your light will pierce the midnight skies.
In every choice, we find our role,
Steered by the compass of our soul.

In whispered laughter, dreams take flight,
A map of love unfolds in sight.
Every step, a note in the song,
That sings of where our hearts belong.

Through storms that come, we'll stand our ground,
In the stillness, our love is found.
With every heartbeat, strong and whole,
Together, we are the compass of our souls.

## **Twilight Embrace**

The sun dips low, the skies aflame,
Whispers of night call out your name.
Stars awaken, in silvery lace,
We find our peace in twilight's embrace.

Shadows dance beneath the trees,
A gentle breeze carries the leaves.
Promises linger in the air,
Wrapped in warmth, without a care.

Nightfall's curtain draws us near,
In this hush, your voice I hear.
Moments linger, softly entwined,
In twilight's glow, our hearts aligned.

Colors fade, yet love stays bright,
Guiding us through the starry night.
With each heartbeat, a story's spun,
In twilight's glow, we are as one.

# **Shining Through the Veil**

A silver glow breaks through the night,
Whispers of dreams take sudden flight.
Moonbeams painting the world's facade,
Shining softly where shadows trod.

Letting go of the day's embrace,
Find strength hidden in gentle grace.
Embers of hope in every gleam,
In twilight's glow, we dare to dream.

Cloaked in silence, yet alive,
The heartbeats echo, and we strive.
With hands outstretched, we catch the light,
Shining through the veil of night.

Weaving stories in the dark,
Each spark ignites an inner spark.
In the stillness, truth reveals,
The beauty this soft night conceals.

## **Lanterns of Hope**

In the silence, lanterns glow bright,
Casting warmth in the depth of night.
Guiding souls through the darkness wide,
With secrets kept, and dreams inside.

Carried forth on gentle winds,
Whispers of love and where it begins.
Each flickering flame a heartfelt wish,
A promise held in the night's soft kiss.

Together walking, hand in hand,
Through unseen paths, we boldly stand.
Embracing shadows, our spirits rise,
Lanterns of hope beneath the skies.

With every step, our fears release,
In the glow, we find our peace.
A journey shared, we find our way,
Lanterns of hope in the break of day.

## **Guiding Flames**

Flickers dance in the midnight air,
Guiding us with a warm, bright glare.
Hearts ignite with a single spark,
Guiding flames light up the dark.

A beacon's call in silence found,
Echoing softly, a sacred sound.
Through tempests fierce and storms so wild,
These guiding flames, they hold us mild.

As shadows twist and shadows play,
Together we'll walk, come what may.
With every step, together we rise,
Chasing dreams beneath starlit skies.

Bound by hope, as spirits soar,
Fires of love will light our core.
In this journey, come feel the grace,
With guiding flames, we find our place.

# The Glow of Sweet Murmurs

In twilight's embrace, whispers rise,
A dance of shadows beneath the skies.
Hearts weave stories soft and low,
In the glow of sweet murmurs, love shall grow.

Beneath the stars, secrets shared,
Each gentle word, a bond prepared.
With every sigh, our spirits align,
A symphony of souls, divinely entwined.

The nightingale sings to the lunar face,
In the stillness, we find our place.
Wrapped in warmth, we silently vow,
To cherish the glow, here and now.

Time drifts softly on the breeze,
Moments linger, aiming to please.
Like fireflies in the velvet air,
Each glow a promise, a love laid bare.

As dawn creeps in, dreams take flight,
The glow of love fades into light.
Yet in our hearts, those murmurs stay,
Guiding us gently along the way.

## **Lanterns of Devotion**

Carried through the night, hearts aglow,
Lanterns of devotion guide us slow.
Each flicker tells tales of our past,
A lighthouse of love, steadfast and vast.

In fields of twilight, we walk hand in hand,
Illuminated paths in a magic land.
The gentle breeze carries your name,
In every spark, I feel the same.

Within the lantern's soft embrace,
We find solace, a sacred space.
Whispers of promises deftly spun,
In the glow of love, we are one.

The night may darken, storms may rage,
Yet our lanterns bright keep turning the page.
Illuminating dreams with a tender light,
In the depths of darkness, love takes flight.

As morning breaks, our lanterns dim,
Yet in our hearts, they forever brim.
Through every shadow, every climb,
We'll carry devotion for all time.

## Echoes of Warmth

In the hearth of silence, warmth ignites,
Echoes of laughter weave through the nights.
With every heartbeat, memories pour,
A tapestry of love, forever more.

Gentle whispers in the fading light,
Remind us of joys, our shared delight.
In every glance, a story unfolds,
In echoes of warmth, our truth is told.

Together we rise like the morning sun,
In the melody of hearts, we become one.
With every breath, we cherish and strive,
In the echoes of warmth, we come alive.

Through autumn's chill and winter's frost,
The echoes remain, never lost.
Wrapped in solace, we find our way,
In the warmth of love, forever stay.

As seasons change, our bond will grow,
In every echo, love's gentle flow.
Through life's journey, forever we'll roam,
In echoes of warmth, we find our home.

## **Kindred Spirits in Illumination**

Two souls aligned in the softest glow,
Kindred spirits sharing the flow.
With every laughter, a spark ignites,
In the depth of night, we chase the lights.

Whispers of hope beneath the stars,
Traveling together, no distance far.
With each encounter, the world aligns,
In illumination, our love defines.

Like constellations sharing their dream,
We dance in rhythms, a radiant beam.
The glow of trust in our gentle gaze,
Together we stroll through life's winding maze.

With every moment, our spirits soar,
Finding the magic in what's in store.
Through trials faced and victories won,
As kindred spirits, we are never done.

The night may darken, the storms may brew,
In our hearts' illumination, we remain true.
Hand in hand, we'll forever fly,
Kindred spirits, love's timeless sky.

## **Starlight Serenade**

In the quiet of the night,
Whispers of dreams take flight.
Stars like diamonds in the sky,
Echoes of hope passing by.

Moonlight dances on the sea,
Carrying wishes, wild and free.
Each twinkle sings a sweet tune,
A lullaby to the silver moon.

Breezes weave through the trees,
Bringing tales of dusk and ease.
Night's embrace, tender and true,
Wraps the world in a velvet hue.

Glimmers of magic abound,
In the hush, peace is found.
Every moment, a spark divine,
In this starlit world, we shine.

Close your eyes, let dreams unfold,
In the night, stories told.
With every heartbeat, know this,
Starlight whispers, not to miss.

## The Embrace of a Thousand Suns

Golden rays begin to rise,
Warming hearts, lighting skies.
Each sunbeam, a tender touch,
Inviting joy, loving much.

Fields bloom with vibrant cheer,
Sounds of laughter draw us near.
Together we dance, brightly spun,
In the embrace of a thousand suns.

Nature's palette, rich and bright,
Colors blend in pure delight.
A canvas painted day by day,
In love's warmth, we find our way.

Hands entwined, we share the glow,
Through every high and every low.
United, our spirits run,
In the embrace of a thousand suns.

As twilight falls, and stars appear,
We still feel that warmth, so near.
Memories spark, like joy begun,
In the embrace of a thousand suns.

## **The Warm Glow of Unity**

Around the fire, stories shared,
In every heart, love declared.
Voices join in harmony,
Creating bonds, a tapestry.

Different paths have brought us here,
In this circle, we have no fear.
Unity shines in every gaze,
A radiant light that truly sways.

Hands uplifted, spirits soar,
Together we are so much more.
In diversity, we find our song,
A melody where we all belong.

Through trials faced, we grow and learn,
In every heartbeat, love will burn.
With every hug, a gentle sway,
The warm glow of unity stays.

As night embraces, stars ignite,
We gather close, hearts full of light.
With every heartbeat, we declare,
In this glow, we're always there.

## Navigating Through Shadows

In the depths where silence dwells,
Whispers echo, casting spells.
Shadows dance upon the walls,
In quiet moments, darkness calls.

Yet through the gloom, a light breaks free,
Guiding hearts to where we see.
With every step, we take a chance,
Navigating shadows with a dance.

Footprints left in waning light,
Show the way out of the night.
Together we face what looms ahead,
With courage born from words unsaid.

Hold on tight, let fears release,
In shared strength, we find our peace.
Through the vale, we find our song,
In unity, we all belong.

The dawn will rise, the light will come,
And in our hearts, we'll find a home.
From shadows deep, we will ascend,
Navigating towards the light, my friend.

With sounds of laughter, joy in tow,
We leave behind the weight of woe.
Together we've journeyed, hand in hand,
Navigating shadows, where hope will stand.

## **A Dance Beneath the Stars**

In the night, where dreams reside,
We twirl and spin, a gentle glide.
The moonlight bathes our whispered sighs,
With every step, the heart complies.

The stars above, they watch and gleam,
As we move lost in a shared dream.
With every glance, the world fades away,
In this moment, forever we'll stay.

The cool breeze carries sweet perfume,
As shadows dance and lovers bloom.
Our laughter echoes in the night,
With every heartbeat, pure delight.

The constellations bear witness true,
To promises made, just me and you.
In silence we're wrapped, a soft embrace,
As time itself slows down its pace.

As dawn approaches, the colors blend,
But in our hearts, the dance won't end.
With every sunrise, we'll find a way,
To keep the stars alive each day.

## **Eternal Flames of Affection**

In the hearth, a flickering glow,
Binding hearts, a love we know.
Through trials faced and laughter shared,
In every moment, how we've cared.

The warmth ignites in whispered nights,
In silence, our souls take flight.
Like embers glowing in the dark,
Our passion fuels the endless spark.

Through storms that rage and winds that blow,
Together strong, just like the fire's flow.
With every heartbeat, flames sustain,
A boundless love that knows no pain.

In every glance, the warmth we find,
A lasting bond that's intertwined.
Through every season, hot and cold,
Our story's worth far more than gold.

As shadows long and twilight comes,
In your embrace, my spirit hums.
Eternal flames forever bright,
In our hearts, love's purest light.

# Candlelit Conversations

In the soft glow of candlelight,
Whispers linger, hearts take flight.
Every secret shared, a gentle thrill,
In quiet moments, we find our will.

With every flicker, the shadows play,
Illuminating what words cannot say.
A glance exchanged, a silent pact,
In this cocoon, we both react.

The glow dances on your face,
Creating warmth in a sacred space.
We speak of dreams, of hopes anew,
Embracing the night that feels so true.

Outside, the world fades to grey,
But here, love guides our way.
With every laugh, with every sigh,
In candlelit warmth, we'll always fly.

As wax drips down, our time's a thread,
We weave the stories left unsaid.
Together we savor each fleeting hour,
In these conversations, love's true power.

## A Symphony of Shimmering Hearts

In the night, a melody unfolds,
With gentle notes of love retold.
We sway together, caught in time,
Each heartbeat sings, a harmony sublime.

The stars twinkle like notes on sheets,
As our hearts dance to rhythmic beats.
In the silence, our spirits soar,
A symphony that yearns for more.

The whispers of the night align,
As you and I perfectly entwine.
With every glance, a new refrain,
In this ballet, we feel no pain.

With strings and winds, the music plays,
Every moment, in endless arrays.
The world fades to a distant hum,
In our embrace, we overcome.

In the crescendo, we find our place,
In the symphony, lost in grace.
Together we'll craft a love that stays,
A masterpiece in endless ways.

# **Guiding Stars of Passion**

In the night sky, dreams align,
Whispers of love, hearts entwine.
Each twinkle a spark, a fleeting glance,
Guiding us forth, in this dance.

Through cosmic trails, our spirits soar,
Chasing the light, forevermore.
With every heartbeat, a story unfolds,
In the warmth of passion, our fate molds.

The constellations hold our key,
To love's vast universe, wild and free.
Beneath their glow, we take our flight,
Bound together, in endless night.

Through storms and shadows, we find our way,
The stars above, they softly say.
In their brilliance, we find the truth,
Guiding our hearts, igniting our youth.

So here we stand, beneath the dome,
The universe whispers, we are home.
With every heartbeat, a promise made,
Guiding stars of passion will never fade.

## Phosphorescent Promises

In twilight's hush, the shadows gleam,
Promises glow like a silver dream.
Each whisper soft, a gentle pledge,
In the depths of night, we won't hedge.

Through the murmur of waves that crash,
We create a bond, unbreakable, brash.
With every glow, our hopes ignite,
Drawing us close in the velvety night.

The world quiets down, as we explore,
Phosphorescent visions as we implore.
With each tender touch, we weave a tale,
In the stillness, our hearts will prevail.

Together we shine, against the dark,
Each promise a fire, a brilliant spark.
Guided by love, through the soft abyss,
In phosphorescent hues, lies our bliss.

So let us dance, under the stars,
Embracing the glow, erasing the scars.
With each heartbeat, we write our fate,
In phosphorescent promises, we celebrate.

## Soft Glimmers of Intimacy

In the quiet night, where secrets hide,
Soft glimmers of love, side by side.
A touch, a glance, in shadows we find,
Intimacy blooms, beautifully blind.

By candle's glow, our laughter sings,
In hushed corners, the heart takes wings.
With every word, a deeper thread,
Weaving our dreams, where none dare tread.

Time softly drifts, like leaves in the breeze,
Moments unspoken, such sweet memories.
In the space between breaths, we reside,
Soft glimmers of intimacy, our guide.

Hand in hand, we traverse the night,
With tender whispers, love takes flight.
In the warmth of silence, our souls unite,
Finding solace in the gentle light.

So let us cherish this fragile dance,
In soft glimmers, our hearts advance.
Bound by the echoes of secrets told,
In intimacy's embrace, we'll grow bold.

## The Firefly's Serenade

In meadows lush, the fireflies play,
A serenade to end the day.
With flickering lights, they weave their song,
Tales of love where we belong.

Among the stars, their dance ignites,
A ballet of dreams on summer nights.
With gentle flutters, in twilight's embrace,
They whisper a tune, a soft trace.

Each glow a promise, a love unfurled,
Dancing in rhythm, hearts in the world.
As twilight deepens, shadows blend,
In the firefly's light, our spirits mend.

Through the dark, they lead us near,
In the symphony of life, we hear.
With every flicker, a memory made,
In the firefly's serenade, dreams cascade.

So let's take flight, in the night's embrace,
Guided by light, in this sacred space.
Together we dance, forever entwined,
The firefly's serenade is love-defined.

Milton Keynes UK
Ingram Content Group UK Ltd.
UKHW021953151124
451186UK00007B/233